The Inside Story
A Journal of Self-Discovery

Susanna Palomares

INNERCHOICE Publishing
15079 Oak Chase Court
Wellington, FL 33414

www.InnerchoicePublishing.com

Editing and graphics by: Dianne Schilling

ISBN – 10: 1-56499-059-4

ISBN – 13: 978-1-56499-059-4

INNERCHOICE Publishing
15079 Oak Chase Court
Wellington, FL 33414

www.InnerchoicePublishing.com

I really ought not to write this . . . but still, whatever you think of me, I can't keep everything to myself, so I'll remind you of my opening words—."Paper is patient!"

But, still, the brightest spot of all is that at least I can write down my thoughts and feelings, otherwise I would be absolutely stifled!

I can shake off everything if I write; my sorrows disappear, my courage is reborn. . . .

—Anne Frank
Diary of a Young Girl

Contents

Introduction

Every child is the keeper of a vast warehouse of "inside stories." Stories about wishes and dreams, friends and pets, exciting and challenging experiences, questions and doubts, fun and work, tough realities and terrific fantasies.

The Inside Story takes children on a guided tour through many of the rooms where their stories are stockpiled. It probes a few corners and brushes away the dust on a handful of memories, encouraging children to capture what they discover in journal form.

Why a Journal? ———

Journal writing is a vehicle for building self-awareness, personal insight, and self-esteem, and is an excellent means of developing language skills, creativity and imagination. Verbal skills, reading comprehension, and written expression are developed through regular writing, while journal drawing stimulates visual thinking and perceiving.

Encouraging children to express their feelings in the privacy of the written word allows the release of pent-up emotions that may have no other outlet. Especially in troubling times, a child can discharge in writing much of the turbulence within or, if words are in short supply, fill the pages with images.

In short, a journal can be a good friend — dependable, patient, and nonjudgmental.

Finding the Pages You Want _____

The Inside Story is intended for use with children in grades three through eight. When used in sequence, the journal pages guide the user to explore past events first, including family history and significant memories. The child is then inspired to peruse current life characteristics and challenges, including friendships, school experiences, values, strengths and weaknesses, likes and dislikes, and goals.

All ninety-three journal pages are grouped by subject area and listed in the table of contents with brief descriptors. This arrangement should make it relatively easy to choose the exercises you wish to duplicate. You may elect to distribute the pages in an altogether different order than they appear in the book, particularly if you are supplementing curricular activities or other events in the classroom or counseling group. Trust your ability to determine which experience is most appropriate at a given time.

Using the Journal Pages _____

I encourage you to be inventive. Use The Inside Story to help your children develop deeper insights into almost any type of experience. Modify the instructions as necessary to increase the effectiveness of a particular page for you and your students. Once the students are comfortable with the process of journal writing, invent new exercises. Invite the children to do the same.

Draw on the experiences of the children to enrich any topic area, discovering and exploring added dimensions related to particular assignments. Personal experiences, beliefs, and insights always make learning more relevant and durable. Topic areas are virtually unlimited, and journal keeping initiated early on often becomes a lifelong commitment.

Duplicate any or all of the pages, and allow your children to write and draw directly on the duplicated pages. Assist the students to bind the pages into book form, so that each one has a complete journal to read and reflect upon at later dates. Creating bound replicas of The Inside Story also encourages the children to pursue the journal process on their own.

If you assign one or two pages at a time, elaborate on the topic a bit before the children actually start working. Field questions, resolve any confusion, and help the children become centered in the activity. After they have finished writing, encourage discussion. The questions given on each page can also be used as a springboard for group discussion.

Establish a Quiet, Respectful Atmosphere ——————

Choose a quiet time and establish a relaxing environment for the journal-writing process. As much as possible, eliminate distractions, noise, and interruptions. Many children enjoy and gain inspiration from music, so consider playing classical or other quiet instrumental selections.

Children who have not been previously exposed to journal keeping or self expression may be hesitant to express themselves freely and candidly. By making journal keeping a safe avenue for creative expression — immune to failure, ridicule, and grading — you are better able to promote writing as a fulfilling and enjoyable activity. A journal is a place to nurture creativity and internal emotional development, not rigid standards of spelling and grammar.

Ideally, journals are confidential. Over time, as the children relax into freely writing and drawing in their journals, the growth and development they experience transfers into other areas of their lives, both academic and personal. If you do choose to occasionally have the students share their journals with others (family, students, you), it is of utmost importance that you view all journals as completely acceptable work just as they are. Journals should never become the subject of grades, lectures, put-downs, or reprimands from anyone — parents, teachers, or other students. If the journals are sent home at any point, include a note to parents discussing the "rules" of journal acceptance.

_____

Protect the Privacy of Every Child

I would like to stress one final point: Individual children will wish at times to keep their journal entries private. Such requests should always be honored. Right from the start, children need to know that they will never be pressured to disclose anything they prefer not to share. Ultimately, the journal is for the individual, and entries are not subject to the approval of others. The journal is a safe place for the children to express themselves freely and honestly. The openness to self-exploration that develops as an outgrowth of privacy is among the most important aspects of journal keeping, promoting in children personal responsibility, self-knowledge, and self-respect.

Journal Pages

If you are an only child, write about what it is like being the only young person in your family. If you have brothers and/or sisters, write about your relationship with each one. What is the birth order of each? Whom do you get along with the best? Whom do you have the most trouble getting along with? Why?

Describe your family. Remember families come in many forms. You might have one or two parents or guardians. You might have step parents or foster parents, or several relatives living in the same house. Whatever your family "looks" like, describe it here with as much detail as you can.

What is your family history? Can you recall any stories you've heard about your family's past? Where did your ancestors come from? Do you have a real "character" or big event in your family's past? Write about your favorite true family story.

What are some things that your parents count on you to do?

What are some things you count on your parents to do?

What are some things you count on yourself to do?

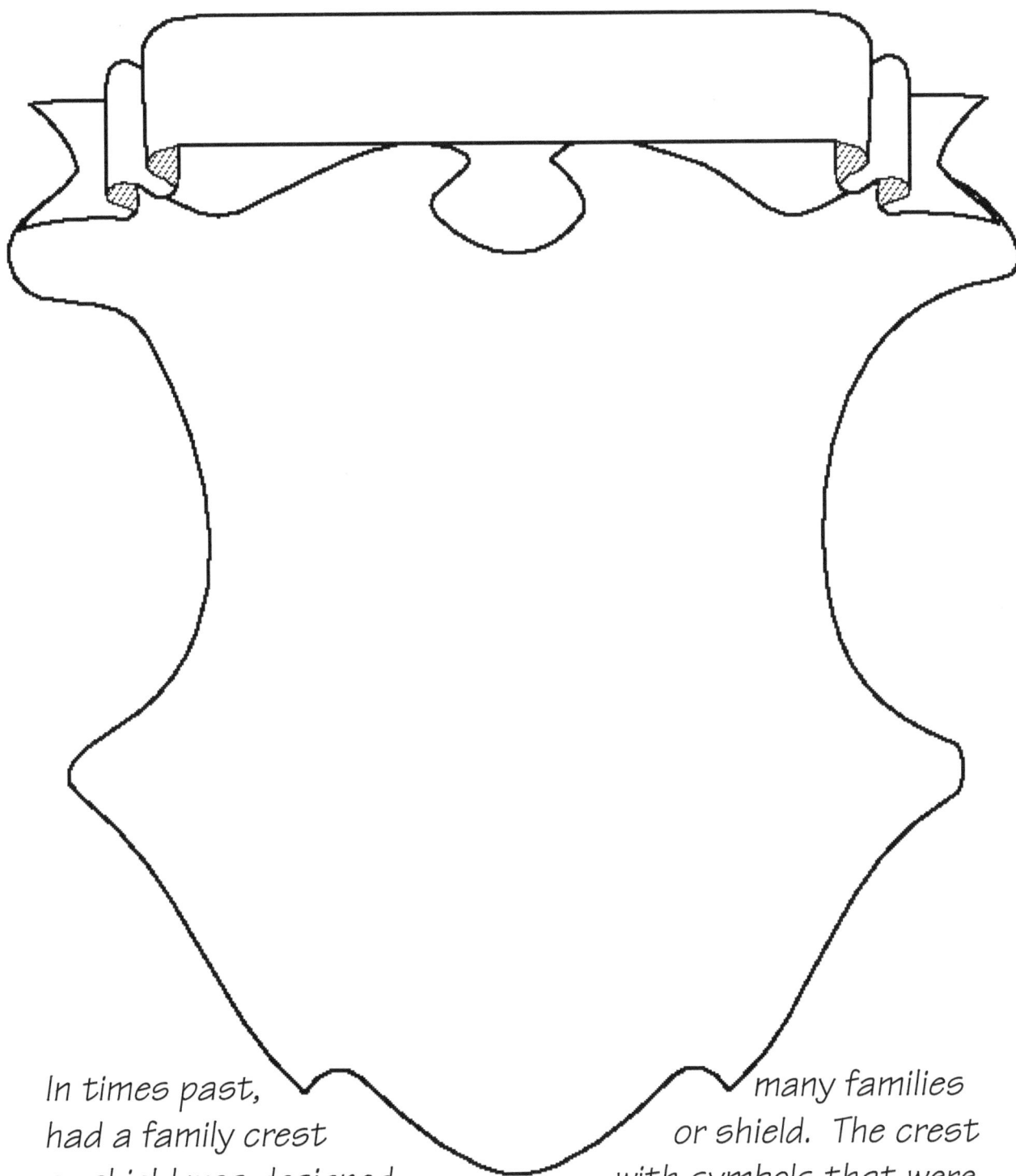

In times past, many families had a family crest or shield. The crest or shield was designed with symbols that were meaningful to the family. Think about your family. What is important and meaningful? Design a crest for your family. Write your family name in the banner across the top and then fill in the shield with designs and symbols.

Think about an enjoyable holiday you and your family have spent together. Draw a picture of the experience.

Now write about your enjoyable family experience.

If you were your parent, how would you set up rules in your house? How would you discipline children who broke the rules?

House
Rules

Try a self-portrait. . . Usually self-portraits are paintings or drawings. If you want your self-portrait to be a painting or drawing, do it here. However, you might like to "write" your self-portrait. You can do that here, too. Maybe you would like to "dance" or "sing" your self-portrait. Can you find a place to do that?

This is me.

What is your earliest memory? Write about this memory using as much detail as possible. As you start writing, more memories may come to you. Keep writing. Use the back of this paper if you need more room. Try to relive the experience in your mind, just as it happened. Write the words "I am . . ." instead of "I was . . ."

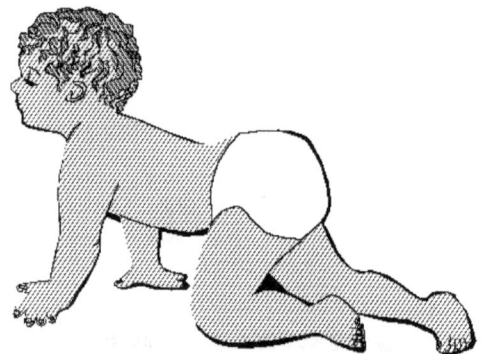

What was the nicest thing anyone ever said to you?
Describe the incident and your feelings.

What was the worst thing anyone ever said to you? Again,
describe the incident and your feelings.

Everybody loves a surprise! What was the best surprise you ever received?

SURPRISE!

Everyone gets hurt once in awhile. Sometimes it's a big hurt. More often it's a little hurt. Describe a time you got hurt. How did the incident take place and what happened to you?

What were the happiest, most joyful times of your life?

	What happened?	How old were you?	Whom were you with?	Where did it take place?
1.				
2.				
3.				
4.				
5.				

Think about a time you were angry with someone. Write about what happened and about your feelings.

If you resolved the situation, write about how you did that. If you didn't resolved it, come up with a positive way in which you might resolve it now.

Who is your oldest friend?

How long have you and this person been friends?

Can you remember the first time you met? Draw a picture, or describe in words, your first meeting.

How has your friend changed since you first met?

How have you changed since you first met?

Make a list. . .

In what ways are you like your friends?

In what ways do you differ from your friends?

Who are the people you count as your friends?

Think of one or two friends that you feel especially close to and write about them. Describe how they look, what their personalities are like, what you do together, and what you like most about them.

Is there someone who was once a good friend, but is no longer? How did the friendship end? Write about what happened, and describe your feelings, too.

If this person came up to you right now, what would you say to him or her?

Have you ever had a fight with a friend? How did the fight start and how did you resolve it?

Did the fight change the friendship in any way? If so, how?

Describe the best time you ever had with a friend. What did you do? Where did you go? See if you can capture in words the parts of the experience that made it special.

You probably have lots of different thoughts and feelings about school. Here are some questions to think about. Write down your thoughts.

What is your favorite thing about school?

What is the most difficult thing you have learned in school?

When do you feel most dumb in school?

When do you feel smartest in school?

...More about school.

What is the best thing that has happened to you in school so far?

Did you learn anything important from this experience?

The trouble with school is . . .

X

X

X

The good things about school are . . .

★

★

★

★

In what ways have you changed since the beginning of this school year?

Do you ever wonder who you are? Think about and answer these questions. Your answers will help describe who you are.

1. How do you feel right now?

2. What do you like about you?

3. What do you dislike about your life?

More

4. How would you change your life?

5. What do you want?

6. What do you need?

What makes you comfortable?

How do you try to bring this comfort into your life?

What makes you uncomfortable?

What do you do to avoid this discomfort?

How do you behave when you are with someone you like?

How do you behave when you are with someone you dislike?

Do bad feelings exist between you and someone else? Who is
the person? _____
How did these feelings get started?

What could happen to change these bad feelings? When you
imagine something happening that might turn this enemy into
a friend, how do you feel?

Nobody is perfect! Everyone gets into trouble once in awhile. Think about a time when you really got into trouble. Write about what happened.

What lesson did you learn from this experience?

Do you think you are a responsible person? Do you also some-times feel a little irresponsible? Write about an area of your life in which you feel very responsible; then write about an area in which you are not as responsible as you would like to be.

Go back and consider both your responsibility and your irresponsibility — what makes the difference?

Draw a picture of yourself in the rectangle (or paste in a photograph). Write a different word on each line that describes you.

_____

_____

_____

_____

_____

_____

_____

_____

_____

What are the things you appreciate most about yourself?
Draw them or write about them on this paper. If you like, do
both — draw and write. Whatever you do, fill the entire sheet!

Describe one thing about yourself that you really like.

Something I Like About Me

Describe one thing about yourself that you would like to change.

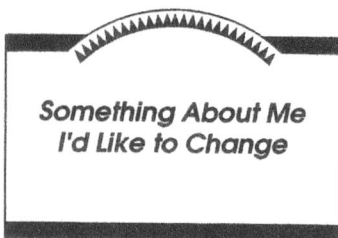

Something About Me I'd Like to Change

Have you ever done something you thought you couldn't do? What was it and how did you do it?

What are your strengths?

How do you use your strengths?

What is one thing that you would like to improve in your life?

Come up with several ideas about how you can make this improvement.

Think of the one word that best describes you.

Explain how you are like this word

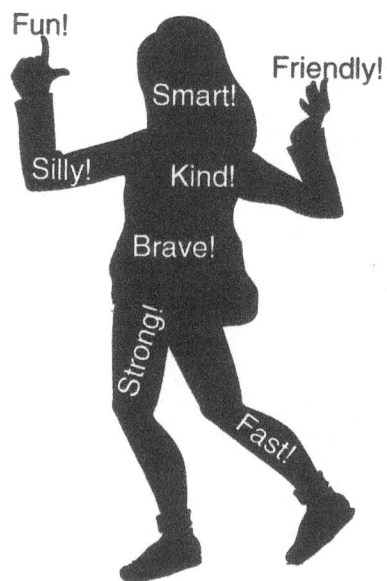
Fun! Silly! Smart! Kind! Friendly! Brave! Strong! Fast!

Draw a picture of yourself right now. (If you prefer, paste in a photo.)

Now, describe yourself here:

How do you feel when you are alone?

How do you feel when you are in a group?

How does your behavior change when you are with others?

What is the nicest dream you ever had?

What is the worst nightmare you ever had?

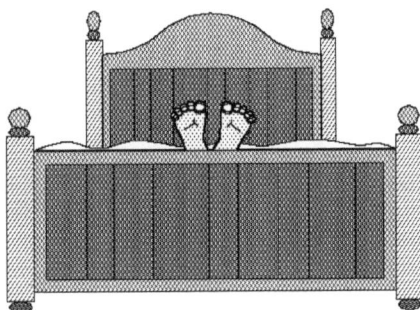

Quickly, without giving it much thought, write down three things under each statement.

I feel . . .

1.

2.

3.

I think . . .

1.

2.

3.

I behave . . .

1.

2.

3.

Now, go back and carefully read what you wrote. Does this tell you anything about yourself? Use the back of this sheet if you need more space.

Focus your attention on the top of your head. Now, concentrate as you move your attention down through your head into your shoulders and then down through your body into your legs, past your knees, into your feet and to the tips of your toes. What is it like for you to really experience your body in this way? Write about what you feel and think.

At what times are you most caring of others?

At what times are you least caring of others?

Are you more caring towards yourself or towards others?

What is the most loving and caring thing you could do for someone else right now?

What is the most loving and caring thing you could do for yourself right how?

If you could change your life in one BIG way, what would it be? After you've written about what you would change, think about how the change would affect the rest of your life. Describe that, too.

What is something that makes you feel insecure? Either write about it or draw a picture of it here:

When you feel insecure, do your feelings affect other parts of your life? Which parts _____

_____

Write about how those parts are affected:

It's often difficult or impossible to change the circumstances that make us feel unhappy; however, lots of times just getting out the words and feelings helps us to feel better. Write about or draw a picture of something that has made you sad.

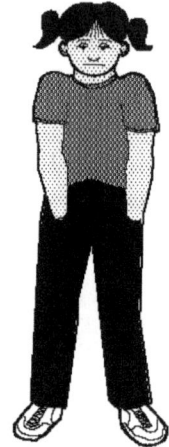

Whom can you talk to about sad feelings?_____
What else can you do to feel better when you have sad feelings?

Everybody has fears — we're just afraid of different things. Some people show their fears more readily than others. Lots of times, it helps to deal with a fear by talking or writing about it. Try that here. Describe a fear you have and what you think might happen.

Have you ever been afraid of something and then got over the fear? Write about a fear you had, and why you think you got over being afraid.

What can you learn from this that might help you get over being afraid of other things?

How do you show that you are angry? Draw a picture of the angry you.

Make a list of all the words you can think of that describe how you feel when you are angry.

_____   _____

_____   _____

_____   _____

_____   _____

_____   _____

_____   _____

_____   _____

What do you usually do when you're angry? Describe the words and actions you use.

When you're really mad and show it, how do other people around you react?

Have you ever said something when you were angry that later you wished you could take back?

Do you know that it is very common for people to displace their anger? This means that although one person or event does something to upset or annoy you, you actually take your anger out on someone or something else. Think of a time when you displaced your anger onto someone (or something) who didn't deserve it. In your mind, try going through the whole event in slow motion, so you can really look at what caused your anger — when you started to feel upset and when you started to behave in an angry way. Pay attention to the other people involved, too. Then, write about it here.

Everyone has hurt feelings at times. Write about a time when someone hurt your feelings. What did the person say or do? What did you say or do? How did you feel as a result of your own actions?

Do you wish you had said or done something different? If so, what?

Write a dialogue between the part of you that has positive thoughts and the part of you that has negative thoughts.

Wow!
Do it! **Great!**
Yes!

It's stupid.
No way! **I hate it.** **Can't!**

Write a dialogue between the happy you and the sad you.

Now, in words . . .
Describe your positive feelings.

Describe your negative feelings.

Have you ever thought that your feelings might have color or shape or form? Draw a picture of your positive feelings on this side of the paper. Then, turn the sheet over and draw a picture of your negative feelings.

What are the mysteries in your life? Do you ever wonder about the meaning of life, or love, or God? How about good and evil, how the universe started and how it will end? Do you wonder how things work and how they were invented? Create a list of unanswered questions that you are curious about. Keep this list and add to it as new mysteries present themselves to you. As you discover answers, try writing about them too. A great place to find answers is the internet. Go there and discover the answers you're looking for.

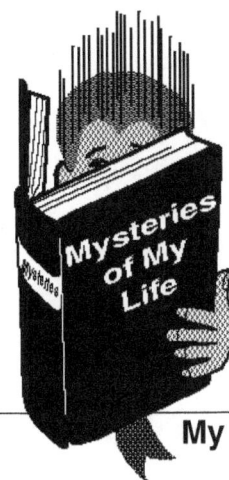

Pretend that today is your birthday. Inside the box is the very best present you could possibly receive. Draw and/or write about it here

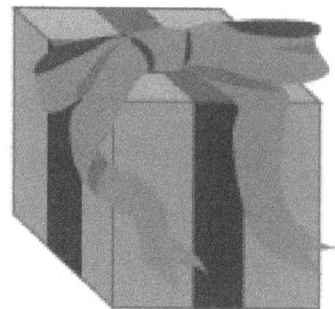

If you could be any animal in the world, what would you be?

_____

Explain why you chose that animal.

Draw a picture of the animal you would be:

My favorite color is

_____

Imagine what it would be like if you woke up one morning and found that everything in the world had turned your favorite color. Describe what it would be like trying to get through the day.

What is your favorite song?

How do you feel when you hear or sing your favorite song?

Why is it your favorite song?

What do some of the words or lines mean to you?

Sometimes it's fun to imagine that toys can come to life. Think about a toy that you have now or had when you were younger and pretend this toy has come to life. What will you and your toy do together and talk about?

*Think of a famous person, either present-day or historical. It can be a real person or a fictional or fantasy character. Whom did you choose?*_____

Write a dialogue between you and the person or character.

What do you think Cinderella might have said to the wicked stepmother after she married Prince Charming?

Dear Stepmother:

Cinderella

If you could say anything to the President of the United States, what would you say?

Dear Mr. President:

Sincerely,

Whom do you greatly admire? Perhaps you admire a friend or relative or a famous person, either living or historical. If you admire several people, go ahead and name them all.

What do you admire about this person (or people)?

Which qualities that you have written about do you also possess?

Have you ever had a peak experience? A peak experience is one that is very special and powerful, and has real meaning and importance to you. Describe the experience with lots of detail, and write about your feelings associated with the experience — both at the time it happened and now.

If you had to go away for a very long time and you could only bring one special possession with you, what would it be? Write about this special possession and why it's important to you.

Everyone has lots of rules to live with. Rules at home, rules at school, and rules that are written into law. What rules do you find the hardest to follow?

What rules do you think are unfair?

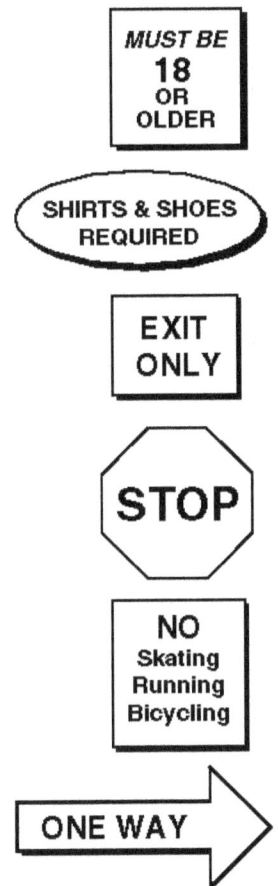

MUST BE 18 OR OLDER

SHIRTS & SHOES REQUIRED

EXIT ONLY

STOP

NO Skating Running Bicycling

ONE WAY

Describe and/or draw something that is very special to you.

If you could have any gift in the world, what would it be and who would give it to you?

How does receiving this gift make you feel?

Who do you think is a wise person?

In what way does this person show you that he or she is wise?

How can you become a wise person?

List the 10 most important things (including people, animals, possessions, traits, and skills) in your life:

1. _____

_____

_____

2. _____

_____

_____

3. _____

_____

_____

4. _____

_____

_____

5. _____

_____

6. _____

_____

_____

7. _____

_____

_____

8. _____

_____

_____

9. _____

_____

_____

10. _____

_____

_____

What is something you would like to have or do right now?

Next week?

Next month?

Next year?

What are you doing that will help you get what you want?

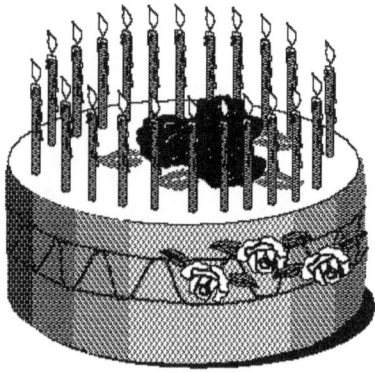

Predict what you will be like when you are 21 years old. Think about as many parts of your life as possible and write about each one.

Look into your future. What do you see? Where do you live? What do you do? What do you look like? With lots of detail and descriptions, write about the future you.

Imagine the ideal you.  In each block, write about
a different part of you, which together with
all the other parts, adds up to
the ideal you.

What is something that you really, really want? Describe it here:

Draw a picture of it here:

What are you doing to get what you want?

What are some things that get in the way of having what you want?

What can you do about the things that get in your way?

How do you feel when you get what you want? Describe your feelings, your thoughts, and your behaviors.

How do you feel when you don't get what you want? Again, describe your feelings, thoughts, and behaviors.

"There's only one corner of the universe you can be certain of improving and that's your own self."

Aldous Huxley

Everyone has things about themselves they would like to improve. Pick one thing you would improve and write about it.

Once you have made this improvement in your life, how would you feel about it.

You're on your own. Write about anything you want.

If your heart is in Social-Emotional
Learning, visit us online.

Come see us at
www.InnerchoicePublishing.com

Our web site gives you a look at all our other Social-Emotional
Learning-based books, free activities, articles, research, and
learning and teaching strategies. Every week you'll get a new
Sharing Circle topic and lesson.

INNERCHOICE Publishing
15079 Oak Chase Court
Wellington, FL 33414